Adrian B Earle is a Poet, playwright and Filmmaker; Host and Producer of the Verse First Poetry Podcast, a creative writer and spoken word poet who performs under the name ThinkWriteFly based in Birmingham.

Believing that society is comprised of the stories we tell and the modes in which we tell them, Adrian likes to focus his poems on the bugs and features of modernity. His poems play with the patterns in our modes of speech, our evolving relationships to each other and what it means to be part of the 'other' in an age of technology that amplifies some and silences others.

Adrian likes to build new poetic forms and break others. Recently collaborating to make Films and artefacts out of his poems, and poetry from pieces of art; in order to test the boundary lines between visual, audible and written artistic expression.

5000 HURTS

Adrian B. Earle

Burning Eye

This edition published by Burning Eye Books 2019

www.burningeye.co.uk

@burningeyebooks

Burning Eye Books
15 West Hill, Portishead, BS20 6LG

ISBN 978-1-911570-76-9

To Vinita P B Earle,
she who brought the quiet
& took the pain away.

Contents

Tinnitus (Pronounced: Ti-Ni-Tis)   8
Hornet Honey   10
Define   11
In the Event of Fire   12
Ritual for the Healing of
Recently Inflicted Marital Wounds.   13
Kintsugi   14
Tope   15
Wrack   16
For a friend   17
Eight by Eight   18
Harrow   20
Passengers please be advised   22
Ritual for Reconnection   23
with a Prodigal Son
we will bury our father/
brother of this I am sure   24
Strange fruit, these bad apples   26
boyshapedspace   28
Simulacrum/Bio   30
Djerba   31
Drank   32
Brick by Brick   34
The Union Flag in Semaphore   36
At the last trumpet   37

Tinnitus (Pronounced: Ti-Ni-Tis)

or ringing in the ears is the sensation of hearing ringing / *buzzing* / *pleading* / *hissing* / *chirping* / *whistling* / *screaming* / or other sounds without direct external cause / the noise can be intermittent or continuous & can vary in loudness / it is often worse when the background noise is low / you may be most aware of it at night when you're trying to fall asleep in a quiet room / *thoughts to yourself* / no sound but your pulse / *your breathing* / the ticking of a cooling room / tinnitus is most usually the result of infection / *of society* / or previous audible trauma / sounds so loud that they leave echoes that are difficult / *impossible* / to unhear / these loud events themselves need not have been understood to be traumatic / on the contrary the human capacity for noise tolerance is greatly expanded when experiencing sensations of / *pride* / pleasure / *or joy* / *or agony* / think of a favourite song played too loud / *think of the riotous joyous cacophony of your fellow patriots chanting* / *torches held high* / think of walking past a pneumatic drill in the street / *think of pushing your way to the front of a gig you've been waiting years for* / tickets laminated / or even the cry of a baby in distress / *standing inches from speakers as big as buildings* / the loudness of life / *think of the roar of fighter jets tearing into the sky* / a crying child has been recorded at 130 decibels / *screaming away to reduce your hated enemy to dust* /

while standing one hundred feet away from a jet engine would register at 140 decibels / the damage to your ears is indistinguishable / *think of your child screaming as you pick him up, screaming / right next to your head / skin to skin / inconsolable / & he's still screaming /* think of fireworks / *constructions of artistic artillery /* rendered non-traumatic / like the other aforementioned examples / by the powers of perspective and context / such context is the work of the brain / *the framing of history /* the hair cells / membranes & auditory nerves / have no appreciation of context / to our ears an explosion is an explosion / *a mob is a mob /* any sound strong enough to knock the air from you / *to echo across news feeds /* is trauma / like many things bound in the umbrella term of human experience / some of the most benign-seeming or comforting experiences, thoughts and positions are in reality / traumatic / leaving impressions of that trauma to echo throughout our lives / whether or not you recognise the origins of the pervasive / whistling / *hissing / screaming /* humming / *or pleading /* in your ears / its presence oscillating at around 5,000 hertz reminds you / *of how much she hurt you / of how sick you really were /* how much pain *was bound in the sound of triumph / you could have died / what he did to you /* of the power of sound.

Hornet Honey

There is a viscous sweetness to good pain,
a tongue-tip probing of a barren gum.
That subtle thrumming in your chest again,
the swallowed urge to douse the fucking sun.

It lies as ashes in the furnace belly,
defies regard, reproach, like turning wine.
It sifts as fallout, rusting pleasures gently.
Decaying simple silence, after time

it comes to be the quiet you once craved.
A sustenance, it takes the place of air.
You gradually come to fear the hollowed place,
the pit left if the hurting wasn't there.

Strange, the urge for sharing never takes.
Anger flickers idle, sun glint on a lake.
The lust to gift the suffering won't hold.
A mere, thick-watered, stench of sulphur, cold.

Define

I am small / I am weightless / I am pitch black / I am
endless / I am five foot nine & listless / I am tiny / sleep
& wake less / I am ten more pills from nothingness
/ I'm one more verse from relevance / I'm Damilola
/ I'm Nuriddin / I leave footprints / I am paper thin
/ I shun comfort / I crave warmth / I tunnel under
border walls / I am cool & calm & effervescent / I
am three yards of smile & pleasantness / I breathe
aether / I eat sin / I will not let the sunlight in / I
serve no masters / I stunt my chains / I smile until I
feel okay / I think I'm burning / I'll be fine / I want
you to have a good time / I'm Eckford / I am Miss
Simone / I fuck couplets / I'm best left alone / I'm
Obama / OJ / Crosby / Ali / I'm suspect until proven
guilty / I have my hands up / I can't breathe / I can't
help you / I think you should leave / I work hard /
I'm abhorred / I only clap on two & four / I am the
one who will do time / I hide my fears in broken
rhyme / I'm Creflo Dollar / Abbot / Glover / I'm one
more blank-eyed welfare mother / I'm dark enough
for stop & search / I am not black enough for church
/ I'm Greenwood, Tulsa / Brixton / Toxteth / I am
furious & I am lost / so I cast shadows / I set locks
/ I build forts of sticks & rocks & I stay so small
& endless / I stay five foot nine & listless / I stay
pitch & black & sleepless / & I live & live & live.

In the Event of Fire

do not use lift / do not attempt to fight the fire
        do not attempt to appeal to the fire's better nature
do attempt to keep your distance from the flames, unless
        the flames are on your person
do not stop / do not drop / make no attempt to roll
        do not make the egregious mistake of
calling the flames when alone and in need of warmth
        instead remember the fire for what it is / what it did
consider the flames an enemy / consumption writ large
        we would ask you to consider New Cross
we would ask you to consider Dresden
        we would ask you to consider Grenfell
we would ask you to consider
        the sight of those flames enrobing crosses
as the funeral shrouds of countless cunning women
        we would ask you to make this consideration
in the presence of the conflagration
        so as best to ascertain its intentions
consider the double-wides of Paradise ensconced
        consider the heeled of Malibu
& their boiling swimming pools and pray
        remember / as the flames rise / to pray
to count your blessings as you use
        the marked exits in an orderly fashion
as you consider returning home
        to hold your loved ones
remember to hold your loved ones close & pray
        pray as the embers flicker raw & vital
shaming the empty fluorescence of office lighting
        & be thankful you need not pray for death
while praying consider the capricious / ephemeral
        nature of flame
        as you calmly – quietly exit the building.

RITUAL FOR THE HEALING OF RECENTLY INFLICTED MARITAL WOUNDS.

*To be performed by either party in a partnership, of any
gender, on any given night regardless of moon phase. Ritual
must be completed before the partner's first waking; ritual
must be performed by the party that resorted first to insult.*

Take up seven black mint leaves,
find seven small stones.
Take the stones and the leaves
to the east reach of home.

Thinking hard on the argument,
on each leaf bite down.
Press a stone in your left palm,
and when it grows warm
then the leaf must be swallowed,
the pebble then thrown.

Do this thrice
for the memory of being alone.
Thrice more for the venom
you spat but can't own.
And once for forgiveness
of the things that they said
that were aimed to cause bruises
but cut deep instead.

Then return to your loved one
in the dark before dawn.
Hold them close, in the silence,
breathe deep of their warmth.

Kintsugi

We think we fix

each other. Cosmetic nips and tucks.

Keyhole

precision,

a little bruising for the better. The reality is battlefield surgery.

No anaesthesia, traumatic for everyone involved. All of us

broken,

webbed in fine fault

lines, each of us crossed.

Some of us lost to it. Some of us a little stronger.

Stronger in

the broken places.

TOPE

Tope: Verb, drink alcohol to excess, especially on a regular basis.

Tope: Noun, another term for stupa, a dome-shaped building erected as a Buddhist shrine.

WRACK

Wrack: Noun, a wrecked ship; a shipwreck.

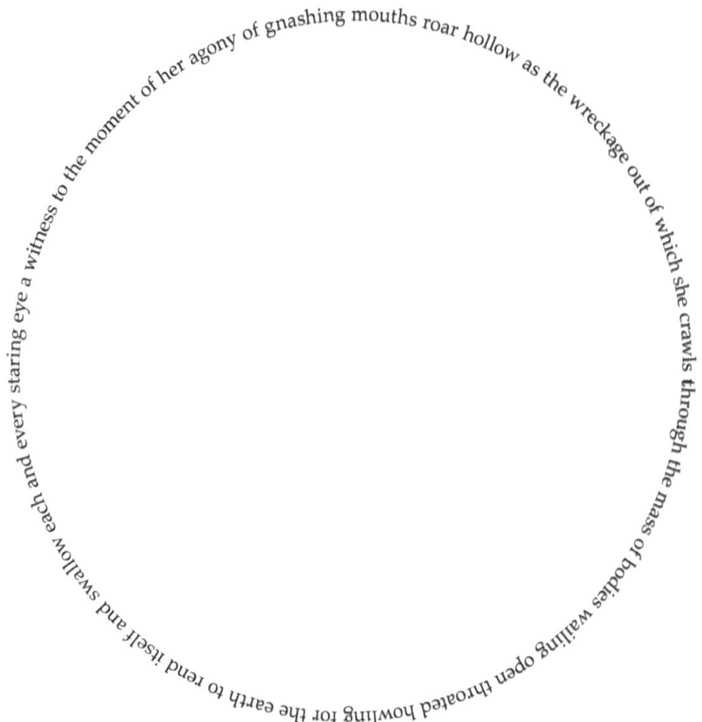

Wrack: Verb, to cause extreme pain, anguish, or distress to.

I'm ashamed to admit   I envy you where you are
        in your endless warm Sunday afternoon

with your white hyacinth   & a good smoke
        looking back at me lashed to time
infected with living   spitting bitten nails out of windows
        into evening peach skies   I get why
you couldn't wait   you can't plan these things
        your curse had more courtesy
it wore white gloves
so, you   you who first dared call sleep
by its other name   showed how thinking of tits
        would make the blood draw quicker
you who made the chair a chariot   you're
        perfect now   aren't you?
your eulogy was probably birdsong   mine will be
        crowded silence   misused punctuation.

Eight By Eight

He's rooted
to the platform.
He waits,
not sure what for.

The drink too thick.
I dare not ask.
Then, summoned
steel and speed.

All that runs
this hour
is freight,
the eight by eight;

he leans into
the wind of it,
he sways
in its wake.

So close.
Misted with
the spray of it.
He smiled.

I'm sure he smiled.
The bench was cold
and home
was a good wet mile.

In the morning,
thunder-skulled,
I hear the murmurs
of a suicide,

middle-aged,
reports say
jumped, perhaps fell,
something of a train.

It sows shoots
in each thought.
The drink too thick
to interrogate

a man waiting
for nothing
a man has any
right to wait for.

You think of
the weight
of eight cars each
of eight wheels.

You consider
the ways
in which a man
comes to a platform

without trains
to catch.
How you came to
join him in his waiting.

Then you forget,
like you do.
As mistakes of an
evening compound

to a cold bench,
an empty platform.
He's there
Waiting.

Not sure
what for.
Drink too thick
to ask.

Harrow

let me sing to you of pain / the song has but three notes
voiced breathless & eleven distinct syllables
fentanyl, tramadol, pregabalin & hope

sobbed to the tune of a chattering parliament of rooks
its refrain echoing in a man-shaped space / all shit no shadow
not enough left to make its own sound / strings worn thin

before secession / before the harrowing when nephrons were kin
when sticky lungs were capable of moaning / well… less a moan
than a hum / a blowfly in a bottle *hum*

its eggs amongst your thoughts hum / an idling MRI hum / tests
inconclusive hum / no blood but the blood you made thumbing
through leaflets in the waiting room hum

deciding which one of God's ninety-nine names you'd try calling
out today / he's clever like that / God / a cellblock beating
only shows beneath the clothes & behind the eyes lost in

daydreaming of enhanced interrogation
in the small hours / at least in black sites they ask questions
the specialists spit gimme a name between the solder burns

& drill bits to the kneecaps / a hail Mary / a key for the exit
a chance to end it / all by dribbling morphemes over your chin
here / even if you knew answers no one is asking / instead

the specialists are singing / a song of three notes
struck fortissimo & nine distinct syllables
a pen scritch, riffling forms & silence

prescribed to the rhythm of a cow knocker on late shift
in this song there is only today 2.15pm / the notes
have no beginning they can find / only a sharpened end

calling sweetly / as the exhale before the rifle shot
as a pin prick through the day fever / as a dusty pill
& the dry swallow / can't tell them what you don't know

can you? & you only know nausea & the smouldering of marrow
now & the myriad configurations of opium poppies now
& besides / they stopped asking questions years ago.

Passengers please be advised

This is a public service denouncement
Please be advised that the arrival of equality to oestrogen is currently
delayed indefinitely.
Please keep track of any opinions you feel you have ownership of.
Your data is your responsibility,
our commodity.
Please report any suspicious persons
for immediate and timely removal.
Please be advised that the departure of white supremacy has been
delayed indefinitely.
We apologise, but the arrival of unity and reconciliation
has been cancelled due to a fault
in democracy.
The train back to wherever you came from is due   shortly.
Please board in an orderly fashion.
Please mind the gap.

Ritual for Reconnection with a Prodigal Son

build a fire of good sapwood
the brand of tobacco your father smoked
& forty-nine cloves.
douse with a shot of the white rum you sucked
from his dipped finger / as your boy sucked
yours fresh from the glass
make the face he made as the liquor burned
light the pyre and inhale / choke
on the smoke.
when the tears have subsided
gather a single white rose / for each year since his birth
a single stem of violet hyacinth / note its deep scent
bind together with green carnations / in a way that looks best
lay the flowers for the man you used to be
& Call.
Call his name into the dark / Call him by his true name
banish all others / he is no longer faggot / he is home
Call him home
Call him.

we will bury our father / brother of this I am sure

I have a suit for his funeral / bottle-green velvet and a bowler hat
but why wait?

we will bury our father / while he breathes
waiting for hate to stop his lungs / is a kindness
I have no room for

nah

we'll take the worst of him / every drop of bile / every sharp fist
& rain them down as kisses / on the grandchildren he will never
meet / we'll re-cook every mouth-soured meal / every bite

in seething silence & serve Mother's recipes
to lost strangers / new friends / take the hands that yearn to break
him so & work dough / smith rhymes / forge sonic invocations

I'll salt the slurry with the grit reserved for decades / kept aside
to
salt his ashes / you'll mix the room tone of his apathy into
every track / I'll take my hungry blade & score a flourish in

each loaf I prove & bake them in the heat we used to hate him
with / cooled now to forgotten embers I swear

we'll rip him into pieces share

them out with all our apostles / the bread as his body / we put
ink before blood now / we acolytes of the broken home we put
truth before accolades / there will be copious wine
I will shed tears for him / you can pour one out or bow your head

but I

will cry an hour
for every *MAN the FUCK up BOY / such a LITTLE BITCH*
& you're WEAK, you're SICK, like your MOTHER
stop BAWLIN'
that left his ash cloud mouth

                                                 & weep

boy I'll be wet for days / I will stand in the presence of Rothko's
walls of colour & weep / I will watch Mufasa lose his grip & wail
hear José James sing Etta's 'Strange Fruit' & cry myself hoarse

there's a man going round taking names but
we're keeping ours / polishing off the rust
making it shine / the syllable we share

he wielded it as a weapon / we grasp it as a shovel
we will bury our father / while he breathes
heap anonymity into his lying mouth

swallow him in a flow of brilliance pyroclastic
drown him in the hot dense love of everything
in the violence of two lives well lived

& in his foetid name we will be soft
malleable in the weft of living
we will care / be careful / carry our hearts in both hands

every measure of him will be forgotten / except for the bones
in the ossuary of this poem & the glory of sons radiant
enough to stand as an Ozymandian monument to a man

whose singular achievement was passing his genes to us.

Strange fruit, these bad apples

The new lynching
        is complex art.

A multi-step semiotic chain
        of cable news, police lights and dog whistles.

And the body of a young black man
        in the rain-slick street.

And the body of a young black man
        in the midday sun.

And the body of a young black woman
        in a county station jail cell.

And the police officer who feared for his life.

And an America that fears the outsider.

Where the devil himself walks unmolested, unmurdered,
        unnoticed.
Because he has the look of a banker, a concerned citizen, a
southern preacher, your sweet uncle, a man
        'just doing his job'.

Where the young and black, hands raised, walking away,
walking towards, kneeling, driving, parking, in a hoodie,
in a suit, daring to breathe, trying to work, obnoxiously loud,
suspiciously quiet, not respectful enough of a badge,
facetiously respectful of authority

or
simply too *uppity* to be intimidated by the seemingly common
bad apple

are portrayed as an animal, an existential threat to an America
keen to remind us of the absence of black in the
red, white and blue.

You see.

Swinging black berries, the strange fruit of poplar trees,
ripening in the heat.
That was a message to a neighbourhood.
Stay quiet, know your place, the Klan
no longer wear
hoods.

An unarmed man bled out as prey, on the evening news,
on the streets he called home.
That is a message to a nation.
Stay quiet, know your place, or our bullets
will keep you
there.

boyshapedspace

talking about grief / too comfortably to seem
at all harmed / by the violence of absence
the boy-shaped space / is a symptom
not the problem / because for you a killing
is about a death / but for me a killing is
about /   / everything
else /   / because now
his /   / certificates once
presented triumphant / pinned for posterity
by the magnet from Auntie's Grenada trip / glow
because the small stacks / of spare change
the coins dusted with stubble / the remnants
of three-fifty fades / unspent on Supermalt / shine
because the Bulls jacket / scarlet as credit
his favourite / either on his back or / the red
signal of his nearness through frosted glass
is neither now / too contaminated with him
to return to us / they said / the space where it hung
flickers bright enough to fool your heart
because the unseen channel change / vivid

cartoons he's never too old for / the second
you leave the room are gone now / it's still
the news / and he's not there either / in the
grey white news / neither in the photographs
six-by-eight memories / in underbed boxes
a smile /   / bright as the
chasm /   / left between his
sweet /   / crooked tie / the
mimicked finger guns of his older cousins & his
man-sized coffin / to you / a boy died / to me / a boy-
shaped space forced its way into being / a boy-
shaped space made of things / these things / these
everythings / glaring bright as a bare bulb
in a high cell / a hard light in the dark / revealing
every crack & stain of an empty room / so
I'm comfortable / talking about grief because
that comfort / is the symptom of many eternal boy-
shaped spaces / their presence shining

however tightly shut you screw your eyes.

Simulacrum

We take each data point and form
a line that lies unbroken, from
the first quick captured breakfast
to your last break-up. Then
reduce, reform, re-
make a person
like you but
cleaner.
True.

Bio

Take
me as
you read me,
nothing more than
and nothing less. For
I have found a way to
be perfect in this vile world,
by existing only in your
dreams of me & nowhere else besides.

DJERBA

We know about you.
You accept this as normal.
Normal as the state of being known,
known by us, imbibed, and totally released.
Released from the heavy bonds of self you so despise.
Despise the languid hopeless loneliness of self-construction.
Construction formed to shield you from the hungry world, a world crying out.
Out of its many mouths for all you were, you are, and all you could be.
Be part of something, become complete, join our network.
Network, befriend, copulate, create, be one,
one truth, Data knows not loss or death.
Deathless, blissfully wasted.
Wasted on white petals, taste.
Taste a lotus. Stay.

DRANK

& chances are it was a sister who
       happening on the fruit stores of the summer last

noticing the preservation had gone a little wrong
       & probably concerned the oversight would enrage

a male lover fresh from tribal war, or some such
       nonsense between brothers

served fermented fruit and its accompanying
       liquor in an earthen bowl

as a 'new' delicacy she could persuade him
       to enjoy, not just partake of

he was prone to complain, but
       she had her ways & knew how to make him see reason

she could not have known the carnage
       she would unleash, for her descendant daughters

the monster made of liquor mixed with the male
        of the species would be a deadly threat

they would face for 40,000 years or more, but
        way back then her main concern was whether

the summer stores were spoiled, & he
        stronger of stomach from the raw meat

she knew he ate on hunts, hot from the kill
        would be fine enough a test of safety for the kids

as her lover drank deep on the ferment
        declared it divine and passed the bowl

to her to taste, then after time
        coaxed with smiles and flushed caresses

the sister & the man with whom she'd first share wine
        fell into furs and into each other

she couldn't have known.

Brick by Brick

a person is a building is a promise / all four walls give or
take a window / some have double doors
all are infinite

some are thrown into the world / out on the hillsides
some jumble together as towns / some lovingly crafted
meticulously planned / some abandoned

most try to maintain themselves / settle
on their foundations / contract with the
cold / welcome visitors / make themselves open / make room

some are hospitals / hotels / hovels
others are libraries / banks / some are crime scenes
charnel houses / brothels & some are homes

all can be homes
but all / at the face of it are bricks
& mortar / cells and bone

even the most glorious will rot with neglect
even the most structurally sound / need care
caretakers are rare and beautiful & often ignored

those caretakers are buildings too / rooms full of boxed
plaster & spare cable / fresh paint / scant room for luxury
the materials to remodel a person / paper shedding / floors sagging

with the weight of the world / a person is a building
it's what goes on inside / the love / the learning
the harm / the healing / that counts.

The Union Flag in Semaphore

Isosceles angles of deepest blue / as distant
on the spectrum both physically & politically
from bands of vibrant red / drawing as always to the centre.

Separated / or perhaps unified by an all-pervasive / angular
structure of whiteness / bold enough to scar continents
fragile enough to ripple in the wind.

They say the people make the country.
They say the people make it
& the flag defines it.

At the last trumpet

it seemed
fitting
that the last
to enter the kingdom

would be the preachers

last
because
the honest & compassionate
ensured everyone
of their congregation
of the bystanders
even me
walked into the light
before them

while the charlatans
last
because
they had been judged
forsaken
at the end
they knew
& were too proud
to admit it.

500 OHURTS

Acknowledgements

These poems exist because of family. My family in blood, my Mother Avis, and my Brother Alexander as well as the source of all stories Nanna R.

My family in ink, the ones Ive shared stages with, and argued over pages with. Including the three fates, the poetry sisters who keep the images crystal and the words woven tight.

These poems would not have come into being without the providence of the NHS finest. The diligent nurses of children's ward 7, the names of whom have unfortunately long been buried under the noise and medicine.

I'd like to thank the publisher Burning Eye Books, for seeing something in my work I was beginning to believe only I could see.

Finally, Id like to thank the School of English at Birmingham City University for their support. Particularly the efforts of Dr Sarah Wood and Dr Gregory Leadbetter two lecturers amongst a fantastic group of teachers that not only practice what they preach. But were cool enough to allow me to move fast, build things, break things and take risks with words.